# The Splendor of Lake Elkhorn

Wynette McKenzie

Publisher's Note: The photographs in this book were taken at Lake Elkhorn in Columbia, MD. All photographs were taken by Wynette McKenzie.

*The Splendor of Lake Elkhorn* © by Wynette McKenzie 2015

Photographs© by Wynette McKenzie

ISBN 978-1-941726-25-9

Five Little Angels Publishing.

All photographs by Wynette McKenzie.

Copyright 2015 by Five Little Angels, LLC.

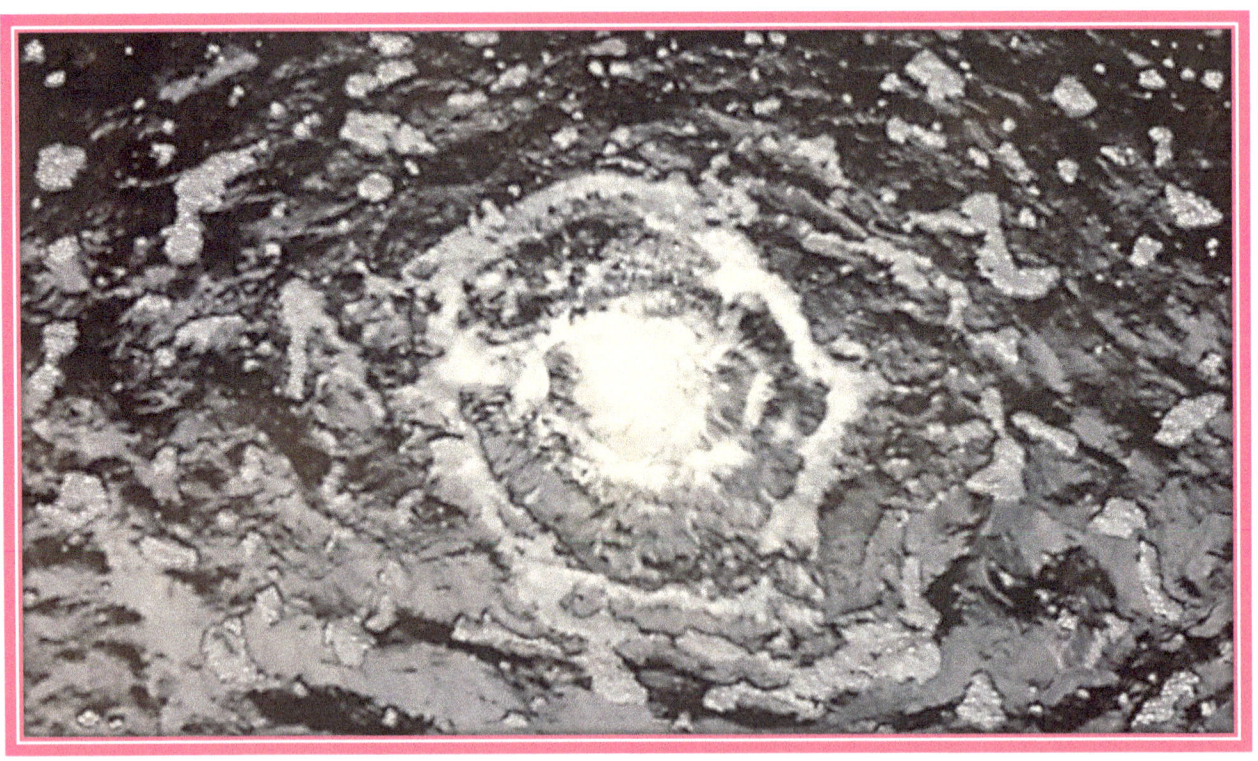

44

86

132

133

# About the Photographer

Wynette McKenzie has been an avid photographer since she was a young girl. She studied photography in New York City and in Maryland while pursuing her higher education degree. She started to take photographs of the magnificent Lake Elkhorn in May 2014.